George Colman, Samuel Foote

The Devil Upon Two Sticks

A Comedy in Three Acts

George Colman, Samuel Foote

The Devil Upon Two Sticks
A Comedy in Three Acts

ISBN/EAN: 9783744661980

Printed in Europe, USA, Canada, Australia, Japan

Cover: Foto ©Thomas Meinert / pixelio.de

More available books at **www.hansebooks.com**

THE

DEVIL UPON TWO STICKS;

A

COMEDY

IN THREE ACTS:

PERFORMED AT THE

THEATRE-ROYAL IN THE HAYMARKET:

WRITTEN BY THE LATE

SAMUEL FOOTE, Efq.

AND PUBLISHED BY

Mr. COLMAN.

ADVERTISEMENT.

SOME copies of spurious impressions of the Cozeners, and the Maid of Bath, having been printed and circulated before the application to the Court of Chancery for an injunction, it has been thought advisable, in vindication of the property of the Editor, as well as in justice to the deceased Author, immediately to commit to the press genuine editions of the two dramatic pieces above-mentioned, together with this Comedy, which had been also without authority advertised for publication.

On inspection of the spurious impressions, it appears, that all the errors of careless and ignorant transcribers are there religiously preserved; and all the additions and improvements, made by the facetious Writer, are omitted. Many instances of this will occur on perusal of those Comedies, and particularly the Cozeners; in which, besides the restoration of several passages always spoken on the stage, the Reader will find a whole scene, at the end of the First Act, and another, still more entertaining and popular, at the beginning of the Third; both which were wholly wanting in the spurious impressions.

Unauthorized publications are not only always detrimental to private property, but commonly prove injurious to the publick: for the copies, being obtained by clandestine and indirect means, are, for the most part, as has happened in the present instance, incorrect and imperfect.

DRAMATIS

DRAMATIS PERSONÆ.

DEVIL,	Mr. Foote.
Sir THOMAS MAXWELL,	Mr. Gardner.
INVOICE,	Mr. Du-Bellamy.
SLIGO,	Mr. Moody.
BROADBRIM,	Mr. Thompson.
OSASAFRAS,	Mr. Egan.
FINGERFEE,	Mr. Hutton.
CAMPHIRE,	Mr. Fearon.
CALOMEL,	Mr. Lings.
DIACHYLON,	Mr. Lewis.
HABAKKUK,	Mr. Pierce.
Dr. LAST,	Mr. Weston.
JOHNNY MACPHERSON,	Mr. Hamilton.
JULEP,	Mr. Palmer.
APOZEM,	Mr. Castle.
FORCEPS,	Mr. Stevens.
SECRETARY,	Mr. Loyd.
PRINTER'S DEVIL,	Mr. Jacobs.

(Doctors.) — bracketed from INVOICE through HABAKKUK.

MARGARET,	Mrs. Gardner.
HARRIET,	Mrs. Jewell.

Servants, &c.

THE

THE
DEVIL UPON TWO STICKS.

ACT I.

A ROOM.

Enter Sir Thomas Maxwell and Margaret.

Sir Thomas.

WHY, the woman is mad! thefe curfed news-paper patriots have fhatter'd her brains! nothing lefs than a fenator of feven years ftanding can conceive what fhe means.

Marg. Why, Sir Thomas, my converfation is neither deficient in order, precifion, or dignity.

Sir Tho. Dignity! and what occafion for dignity in the common concerns of my houfe? why the deuce can't you converfe like the reft of the world? If you want money to pay off my bills, you move me for further fupplies; if I turn away a fervant, you condemn me for fo often changing my miniftry; and becaufe I lock up my daughter, to prevent her eloping with the paltry clerk of a pitiful trader, it is forfooth an invafion of the Bill of Rights, and a mortal ftab to the great Charter of Liberty.

Marg. As Serjeant Second'em faid in the debate on the corn-bill, "Then why don't you chufe "better ground, brother, and learn to enlarge "your bottom a little? Confider, you muft draw "the line of liberty fomewhere; for ifthefe rights "belong"——

Sir Tho. Mercy on us!

Marg.

Marg. But indeed, my dear brother, you are got quite out of your depth: Woman, I tell you, is a microcofm, and rightly to rule her requires as great talents, as to govern a ftate. And what fays the Aphorifm of Cardinal Polignac? " If " you would not have a perfon deceive you, be " careful not to let him know you miftruft him!" and fo of your daughter.

Sir Tho. Mrs. Margaret Maxwell, beftow your advice where it is wanted! Out of my depth! a likely ftory indeed, that I, who am fixed here in a national truft, appointed guardian of the Eng- lifh intereft at the court of Madrid, fhould not know how to manage a girl!

Marg. And pray, Mr. Conful, what informa- tion will your ftation afford you? I don't deny your knowledge in export and import, nor doubt your fkill in the difference between wet and dry goods; you may weigh with exactnefs the bal- lance of trade, or explain the true fpirit of a treaty of commerce; the furface, the mere fkimmings of the political pot!

Sir Tho. Mighty well!

Marg. But had you, with me, traced things to their original fource; had you difcover'd all focial fubordination to arife from original compact; had you read Machiavel, Montefquieu, Locke, Bacon, Hobbes, Harrington, Hume; had you ftudied the political teftaments of Alberoni and Cardinal Richlieu——

Sir Tho. Mercy on us!

Marg. Had you analized the Pragmatick Sanc- tion, and the family-compact; had you toil'd thro' the laborious page of the Vinerian profeffor, or eftimated the prevailing manners with the Vicar of Newcaftle; in a word, had you read

Amicus

Amicus upon Taxation, and Inimicus upon Re-
prefentation, you would have known———

Sir Tho. What?

Marg. That, in fpite of the frippery French
Salick laws, woman is a free agent, a noun
fubftantive entity, and, when treated with confidence——

Sir Tho. Why, perhaps, fhe may not abufe it:
But ftill, my fage fifter, it is but a *perhaps*; now
my method is certain, infallible; by confining
her, I can't be deceived.

Marg. And pray, Sir, what right have you
to confine her? look in your Puffendorff! tho'
born in Spain, fhe is a native of England; her
birth-right is liberty—a better patrimonial eftate
than any of your defpotic countries could give
her.

Sir Tho. Zooks, you would tire the patience
of Job! Pray anfwer me this; is Harriet my
daughter?

Marg. What then? for that ineftimable bleffing
fhe is not beholden to you; nor can you, tho' a
father, with reafon, juftice, or law, take it from
her.

Sir Tho. Why, Margaret, you forget where you
are! This, child, is the town of Madrid; you are
amongft a fage, fteady people, who know and
revere the natural rights of a parent.

Marg. Natural rights! Can a right to tyrannize
be founded in nature?

Sir Tho. Look'ee, Margaret! you are but lofing
your time; for unlefs you can prevail on Count
Wall, or the prefident of Caftille, to grant you a
Habeas, why Harriet fhall ftay where fhe is.

Marg. Ay, ay, you know where you are; but,
if my niece will take my advice, the juftice that

is

is denied to her here, she will instantly seek for elsewhere.

Sir Tho. Elsewhere? hark you, sister! is it thus you answer my purpose in bringing you hither? I hoped to have my daughter's principles form'd by your prudence; her conduct directed by your experience and wisdom.

Marg. The preliminary is categorically true.

Sir Tho. Then why don't you abide by the treaty?

Marg. Yes; you have given me powerful motives.

Sir Tho. But another word, madam: as I don't chuse that Harriet should imbibe any more of your romantic republican notions, I shall take it as a great favour if you would prepare to quit this country with the first opportunity.

Marg. You need not have remonstrated; a petition would have answered your purpose: I did intend to withdraw, and without taking leave; nor will I reside on a spot where the great charter of my sex is hourly invaded! No, Sir Thomas; I shall return to the land of liberty! but there expect to have your despotic dealings properly and publicly handled.

Sir Tho. What, you design to turn author?

Marg. There's no occasion for that; liberty has already a champion in one of my sex: The same pen that has dared to scourge the arbitrary actions of some of our monarchs, shall do equal justice to the oppressive power of parents!

Sir Tho. With all my heart.

Marg. I may, perhaps, be too late to get you into the historical text; but, I promise you, you shall be soundly swinged in the marginal note.

Enter a Servant, who whispers Sir Thomas.

Sir Tho. What! now?

Serv. This instant.

Sir Tho. How did he get in?

Serv. By a ladder of ropes, dropt, I fuppofe, by Mifs Harriet from the balcony.

Sir Tho. That way, I reckon, he thinks to retreat; but I fhall prevent him? Here, Dick, do you and Ralph run into the ftreet, and front the houfe with a couple of carbines; bid James bring my toledo; and let the reft of the fellows follow my fteps!

Marg. Hey-day! what can be the meaning of this civil commotion?

Sir Tho. Nothing extraordinary; only the natural confequence of fome of your falutary fuggeftions.

Marg. Mine, Sir Thomas?

Sir Tho. Yes, yours, fifter Margaret!

Marg. I don't underftand you.

Sir Tho. Oh, nothing but Harriet making ufe of her great natural charter of liberty, by letting young Invoice, Abraham Indigo's clerk, by the means of a ladder of ropes, into her chamber.

Marg. I am not furprized.

Sir Tho. Nor I neither.

Marg. The inftant your fufpicions gave her a guard, I told her the act was tantamount to an open declaration of war, and fanctified every ftratagem.

Sir Tho. You did? mighty well, madam! I hope then, for once, you will approve my proceedings; the law of nations fhall be ftrictly obferved; you fhall fee how a fpy ought to be treated, who is caught in the enemy's camp!

Enter Servant with the toledo.

Oh, here's my trufty toledo. Come, follow your leader! [*Exit with Servants.*

Marg. Oh, Sir, I fhall purfue, and reconnoitre your motions; and tho' no cartel is fettled between;

tween you, take care how, you infringe the
jus gentium.   [*Exit Marg,*

Another chamber. Harriet and Invoice discovered.

Har. Are you sure you were not observed?

Inv. I believe not.

Har. Well, Mr. Invoice, you can, I think, now
no longer doubt of my kindness; tho', let me tell
you, you are a good deal indebted for this early
proof of it, to my father's severity.

Inv. I am sorry, madam, an event, so happy for
me, should proceed from so unlucky a cause: But
are there no hopes that Sir Thomas may be
softened in time?

Har. None: He is, both from nature and
habit, inflexibly obstinate. This too is his favourite foible; no German baron was ever more
attached to the genealogical laws of alliance
than he: Marry his daughter to a person in
trade? no! Put his present favourite out of the
question, he can never be brought to submit to it.

Inv. Dear Miss Harriet, then why will you
hesitate? there can be no other alternative; you
must either submit to marry the count, or by
flight escape from the——

Har. No, Mr. Invoice, not till the last necessity
drives me. Besides, where can we go? how sub-
sist? who will receive us?

Inv. *The world is all before us where to chuse;*
and, as we fly from oppression, *Providence our guide.*

Har. The world, Mr. Invoice, is but a cold
kind of common; and, as to Providence, let
us first be sure we deserve its protection.——
[*A noise without.*] Bless me! don't I hear some
bustle below?

Inv. Madam!

Har,

Har. Hufh! my father, as I live! I fear, Mr. Invoice, you are difcovered.

Inv. No, furely!

Sir Tho. [*without.*] Have you fecured all the pofts?

Serv. [*without.*] All, Sir.

Sir Tho. Both the front and the rear?

Serv. Both.

Har. Loft, paft redemption!

Sir Tho. Then advance! now let us unharbour the rafcal!

Har. What can we do?

Sir Tho. Come, madam, open your doors!

Har. The balcony, quick, Mr. Invoice, the balcony!

Sir Tho. Unlock, Mrs. Minx! your minion is difcovered.

Inv. A couple of fellows ftand below, with their pieces pointed directly againft it.

Sir Tho. What, then, you will compel us to batter?

Har. The whole houfe is furrounded! how can you efcape?

Inv. Where will this window conduct us?

Har. To the leads that join our houfe to the chymift's.

Inv. To the leads? it is but a ftep; there is no danger.

Har. Then inftantly fly! you have every thing to fear from my father.

Sir Tho. John, fetch the mattock and crow!

Inv. And leave my Harriet behind me?

Har. Secure yourfelf, and abandon me to my fate.

Inv. No, madam, that I will never do; I'll dare your father's utmoft refentment,

Sir

Sir Tho. Where is that rafcal loitering?

Har. Then you are loft!

Inv. Would my Harriet accompany my flight—

Har. Can you defire it?

Inv. I do, I do; my deareft angel, I do! By all that's facred, your honour fhall be as fecure with me as in the cell of a faint!

Har. But character, decency, prudence——

Inv. The occafion, the danger, all juftify—

Sir Tho. Oh, what, you are come at laft.

Inv. Determine, my life! You have but a moment—

Har. Should you, Mr. Invoice, deceive me—

Inv. When I do, may my laft hope deceive me!

Har. It is a bold, a dangerous ftep!

Inv. Fear nothing, my love!

> *Advances to the window, and gets out.*

Sir Tho. Drive at the pannel.

Marg. [*without.*] I enter my proteft!

Sir Tho. And I will enter the room!

Inv. Now leap; all is fafe.

> *Harriet gets out at the window.*

Sir Thomas, adieu!

Sir Tho. Wrench open the lock!

Marg. Ay, do, at your peril!

Sir Tho. Down with the door!

Marg. Then you fhall all be fwingingly foufed. Produce your authority.

Sir Tho. Mine!

Marg. You have none; not fo much as the fanction of a general warrant.

Sir Tho. What, then, I fee I muft do it myfelf; There it goes! Pretty law indeed, to lock a man out of his own houfe!

> *Enter*

Enter Sir Thomas, Margaret, and Servants.

Now, Mrs.—Heyday! what are become of the parties? vanifhed?

Marg. Deceived by your fpies! no uncommon thing, brother, for a blundering general.

Sir Tho. You are fure you faw him come in?

Serv. Certain, Sir Thomas.

Sir Tho. Then I warrant we will ferret them out. Come, lads! let not a corner efcape you!
[*Exeunt Sir Tho. and Servants.*

Marg. I fhall wait on your motions, and bring up the rear. [*Exit.*

Scene changes to the Chymift's.

Enter Invoice and Harriet, through the fafh.

Inv. Safely landed, however.

Har. Are you fure you are not purfued?

Inv. Not a foul: Never fear! they will hardly venture this road.

Har. What a ftep have you induced me to take! to what diftrefs and difficulties have I expofed myfelf!

Inv. Banifh your fears, and let us look forward, my love.

Har. Nay, I have gone too far to retreat. Well, Sir, what is next to be done?

Inv. The Spaniards are naturally generous; perhaps, upon hearing our ftory, the owner of the houfe may lend his affiftance. This, I fuppofe, is the Laboratory, and this door leads to the fhop.

Devil [*in a bottle.*] Heigh-ho!

Har. Who is that?

Inv. That! where?

Har. Did not you hear a voice?

Inv.

Inv. None. Fancy, my love; only your fears.

Devil. Heigh-ho!

Har. There again!

Inv. I hear it now.—Who is there?

Devil. Me.

Inv. Me? he speaks English! Who and where are you?

Devil. Here in this bottle; where I have been cork'd up for these six months.

Inv. Cork'd up in a bottle! I never heard of such a thing in my life, unless, indeed, in the Haymarket once.—Cork'd up in a bottle, d'ye say?

Devil. Ay; by the master of this house, a magician.

Inv. A magician! Why then you are a spirit, I suppose.

Devil. You are right; I am the Devil.

Har. Mercy on us!

Devil. Don't be terrified, Miss: You remember the old proverb, " The Devil is not so black " as he is painted."

Inv. Well, but Sir—

Devil. A truce to your questions, my good Sir, for the present!—Consider, ramm'd up in this narrow compass, I can't be much at my ease; now if you will but break the bottle before you on the floor——

Har. For heaven's sake, Mr. Invoice, take care what you do.

Devil. Why, my pretty Miss, what risque do you run? your affairs can hardly be changed for the worse.

Har. That's true, indeed!

Devil. Believe me, Miss, as matters stand, we can be of mutual use: Your lover may deliver me

from

from prifon, and I can prevent you both from going into confinement.

Inv. What fays my Harriet? fhall I rely on
the gentleman's word?

Devil. Do, madam! I am a Devil of honour.
Befides, you have but a little time to confider ;
in lefs than five minutes, you will have the Conful and all his crew in the houfe.

Inv. Nay, then—Pray which is the bottle?

Devil. That in the middle, right before you.

Inv. There it goes!

    [*He breaks the bottle, and Devil rifes out*
        of it. Thunder.

Har. Oh, what a——

Devil. I am not furprized, Mifs, that you are a
little fhocked at my figure : I could have affumed
a much more agreeable form; but as we are to be
a little better acquainted, I thought it beft to
quit all difguife and pretence; therefore, madam,
you fee me juft as I am.

Har. I am fure, Sir, you are ve—ve—very
agreeable.

Devil. Yo—yo—you are pleafed to compliment,
madam.—Come, anfwer me fincerely ; am I fuch
a being as you expected to fee?

Har. Really, Sir, I can hardly fay what I expected to fee.

Devil. I own it is a puzzling queftion; at leaft,
if the world does us juftice in the contradictory
qualities they are pleafed to afford us.

Inv. You will forgive me, if I don't underftand
you.

Devil. Why, for all their fuperlative epithets,
you cannot but fee how much men are beholden
to us ; by our means it is that you meafure the
extent both of your virtues and vices.

Inv.

Inv. As how?

Devil. As thus: In defcribing your friends, or your foes, they are *devilifh* rich, *devilifh* poor, *devilifh* ugly, *devilifh* handfome; now and then, indeed, to vary the mode of converfing, you make a little free with our condition and country, as, *hellifh* dull, *damn'd* clever, *hellifh* cold; Pfha! how *damn'd* hot it is!

Inv. True, Sir, but I confider this as a rhetorical figure, a manner of fpeaking devifed and practifed by dulnefs, to conceal the lack of ideas, and the want of expreffions.

Devil. Partly that, I confefs: Not but there is fome truth in the cafe; for at different times we have the power, and do affume the various forms, you affign us.

Inv. We? I obferve you always make ufe of the plural; is that, Sir, by way of diftinction, or, is your family pretty large and extenfive?

Devil. Multitudinous as the fands on the beach, or the moats in a fun beam: How the deuce elfe do you think we could do all the bufinefs below? Why, there's fcarce an individual amongft you, at leaft of any rank or importance, but has five or fix of us in his train.

Inv. Indeed!

Devil. A little before I got rammed in that phial, I had been for fome time on very hard duty in this part of the world.

Inv. Of what kind?

Devil. The Dæmon of Power and I had long laid fiege to a fubject, the man a grandee; I was then a popular fpirit, and wore the mafk of a patriot; at different times, we poffeffed him by turns; but, in the midft of a violent ftruggle (by which means I got lame on this leg, and obtained

tained the nick-name of the Devil Upon Sticks),
the Dæmon of Vanity, a low under-ftrapper
amongſt us, held over his head a circle of gold,
with five knobs on the top, and, *whew!* flew
away with our prize in an inſtant.

Inv. Under-ſtrapper! what, are there different
ranks and orders amongſt you?

Devil. Without doubt.

Inv. And pray, Sir—I hope, no offence;
but I would not be wanting in proper refpect—
are you, when at home, of condition? or how
muſt I——

Devil. You mean, am I a Devil of faſhion,
or one of the bafe born?

Inv. I do.

Devil. I have no reaſon to be aſhamed of my
family.

Inv. I don't doubt it.   You will forgive me,
if I make a miſtake: Perhaps, my lord Lucifer.

Devil. Who?

Inv. Lord Lucifer.

Devil. *Lord* Lucifer? how little you know
of our folks! Lucifer a *lord!* Why, that's the
meaneſt rafcal amongſt us.

Inv. Indeed!

Devil. Oh, a paltry mechanic! the very
genius of jobbing! a mere Bull and Bear
booby; the patron of lame ducks, brokers,
and fraudulent bankrupts.

Inv. You amaze me! I vow I always thought
him a principal agent.

Devil. He! Not at all. The fellow, indeed,
gave himſelf fome airs of importance, upon
following the camp, and having the Contractors
and Commiffaries under his care; but that affair,
you know, clofed with the war.

B   *Inv.*

Inv. What, then, are they now entirely out of his hands?

Devil. Yes; quite out of his: He only suggested their *cent. per cent.* squeezings, and prompted the various modes of extortion and rapine: But, in his room, they have six or seven Dæmons a-piece, to direct the dissipation of their ill-gotten wealth.

Inv. Indeed!

Devil. Poor Lucifer, it is all over with him! if it were not for the fluctuation of India, an occasional lottery, or a contested election, the Alley would be empty, and Lucifer have as little to do as a pickpocket when the playhouses are shut.

Inv. Perhaps, Sir, then your name may be Belzebub?

Devil. He? worse and worse! Not a devil that has the least regard to his character would chuse to be seen in his company: Besides, it is the most petulant, waspish, quarrelsome cur——But no wonder; he is the imp of chicane, and protects the rotten part of the law.

Inv. Then he, at least, has employment enough.

Devil. Yes, during the Term, he has a good deal to do: He is the parent of quibbles, the guardian of pettifoggers, bad bail, and of bailiffs: the supporter of *alibi's* the source of sham pleas, the maker and finder of laws, the patron of perjury, and a sworn foe to all trials by jury! Not long ago, though, my gentleman was put to his shifts.

Inv. How was that?

Devil. The law had laid hold of an old friend of his, for being too positive as to a matter of fact; evidence, evasion, protraction, pleas, every

art,

art, was employed to acquit him, that the moft confummate fkill could fuggeft; but all to no purpofe.

Inv. That was ftrange.

Devil. Beyond all belief; he could have hang'd a dozen innocent people, with half the pains that this paltry perjury gave him.

Inv. How came that about?

Devil. Why—I don't know—he had unfortunately to do with an obftinate magiftrate, who bears a mortal hatred to rogues, and whofe fagacity could not be deceived. But, however, tho' he was not able to fave his friend from the fhame of conviction (a trifle, which he indeed but little regarded), yet he had the addrefs to evade, or at leaft defer, the time of his punifhment.

Inv. By what means?

Devil. By finding a flaw.

Inv. A flaw! what's a flaw?

Devil. A legal loop-hole, that the lawyers leave open for a rogue now and then to creep through, that the game mayn't be wholly deftroy'd.

Inv. Provident fportfmen! Would it not be too much trouble to favour me with this particular inftance?

Devil. Not at all. Why, Sir, when matters grew defperate, and the cafe was given over for loft, little Belzy ftarts up in the form of an able practitioner, and humbly conceived, that his client could not be convicted upon that indictment; forafmuch as therein he was charged with forfwearing himfelf N O W; whereas it clearly appeared, by the evidence, that he had only forfworn himfelf T H E N: If, indeed, he had been

indicted

indicted generally, for committing perjury *now* AND *then*, proofs might be produced of any perjury that he may have committed; whereas, by limiting the point of time to the *now*, no proofs could be admitted as to the *then:* So that, with submiffion, he humbly conceived, his client was clearly abfolved, and his character as fair and as fpotlefs as a babe that's juft born, and immaculate as a fheet of white paper.

Inv. And the objection was good?

Devil, Fatal; there was no getting rid of tho flaw.

Inv. And the gentleman——

Devil. Walks about at his eafe; not a public place, but he thrufts his perfon full in your face,

Inv. That ought not to be; the contempt of the Public, that neceffary fupplement to the beft-digefted body of laws, fhould in thefe cafes be never difpenfed with.

Devil. In days of yore, when the world was but young, that method had merit, and the fenfe of fhame was a kind of a curb; but knaves are now fo numerous and wealthy, they can keep one another in countenance, and laugh at the reft of the world.

Inv. There may be fomething in that.—— Well, Sir, I have twice been out of my guefs; will you give me leave to hazard a third? Perhaps you are Belphegor, or Uriel?

Devil. Neither. They too are but diminutive devils: The firft favours the petty, pilfering frauds; he may be traced in the double fcore and foap'd pot of the publican, the allum and chalk of the baker, in the fophifticated mixtures of the brewers of wine and of beer, and in the falfe meafures and weights of them all.

Inv.

Inv. And Uriel?

Devil. He is the Dæmon of quacks and of mountebanks; a thriving race all over the world, but their true seat of empire is England: There, a short sword, a tye, and a nostrum, a month's advertising, with a shower of handbills, never fail of creating a fortune. But of this tribe I forefee I shall have occasion to speak hereafter.

Inv. Well, but, Sir——

Devil. Come, Sir, I will put an end to your pain; for, from my appearance, it is impossible you should ever guess at my person.—Now, Miss, what think you of Cupid?

Har. You? you Cupid? you the gay god of love?

Devil. Yes; me, me, Miss!—What, I suppose you expected the quiver at my back, and the bow in my hand; the purple pinions, and filletted forehead, with the blooming graces of youth and of beauty.

Har. Why, I can't but say the poets had taught me to expect charms——

Devil. That never existed but in the fire of their fancy; all fiction and phrenzy!

Inv. Then, perhaps, Sir, these creative gentlemen may err as much in your office, as it is clear they have mistaken your person.

Devil. Why, their notions of me are but narrow. It is true, I do a little business in the amorous way; but my dealings are of a different kind to those they describe.—My province lies in forming conjunctions absurd and preposterous: It is I that couple boys and beldames, girls and greybeards, together; and when you see a man of fashion lock'd in legiti-

mate

mate wedlock with the ftale leavings of half the fellows in town, or a lady of fortune fetting out for Edinburgh in a poft-chaife with her footman, you may always fet it down as fome of my handywork. But this is but an inconfiderable branch of my bufinefs.

Inv. Indeed!

Devil. The feveral arts of, the drama, dancing, mufick, and painting, owe their exiftence to me: I am the father of fafhions, the inventor of *quints, trente, quarante,* and hazard; the guardian of gamefters, the genius of gluttony, and the author, protector, and patron of licentioufnefs, lewdnefs, and luxury.

Inv. Your department is large.

Devil. One time or other I may give you a more minute account of thefe matters; at prefent we have not a moment to lofe: Should my tyrant return, I muft expect to be again cork'd up in a bottle. [*Knocking.*] And hark! it is the conful that knocks at the door; therefore be quick! how can I ferve you?

Inv. You are no ftranger, Sir, to our diftrefs: Here, we are unprotected and friendlefs; could your art convey us to the place of our birth—

Devil. To England?

Inv. If you pleafe.

Devil. Without danger, and with great expedition. Come to this window, and lay hold of my cloak.—I have often refided in England: At prefent, indeed, there are but few of our family there; every feventh year, we have a general difpenfation for refidence; for at that time the inhabitants themfelves can play *the devil* without our aid or affiftance.—Off we go! ftick faft to your hold! [*Thunder, Exeunt.*

ACT

A C T II.

A STREET IN LONDON.

Enter Devil, Invoice, and Harriet.

Devil.

WELL, my good friends, I hope you are not difpleafed with your journey.

Inv. We had no time to be tired.

Har. No vehicle was ever fo eafy.

Devil. Then, by you mortals what injuftice is done us, when every crazy, creaking, jolting, jumbling coach, is called *the devil of a carriage.*

Inv. Very true.

Devil. Oh, amongft you we are horridly ufed— Well, Sir, you now fee I am a Devil of honour, and have punctually obeyed your commands: But I fha'n't limit my gratitude to a literal compliance with our compact; is there any thing elfe for your fervice?

Inv. Were I not afraid to trefpafs too much on your time——

Devil. A truce to your compliments! Though they are the common change of the world, we know of what bafe metal the coin is compofed, and have cried down the currency: Speak your wifhes at once.

Inv. England, Sir, is our country, it is true; but Mifs Maxwell being born abroad, and my leaving it young, have made us both as much ftrangers to it manners and cuftoms, as if you had fet us down at Ifaphan or Delhi: Give us, then, fome little knowledge of the people with whom we are to live.

Devil. That tafk, young gentleman, is too much even for the Devil himfelf! Where liberty reigns,

and

and property is pretty equally fpread, indepen-
dence and pride will give each individual a pecu-
liar and feparate character: When claffed in pro-
feffions, indeed, they then wear fome fingular
marks that diftingufh them from the reft of their
race; thefe it may be neceffary for you to know.

Inv. You will highly oblige me.

Devil. And at the fame time that I am fhewing
you perfons, I will give you fome little light into
things. Health and property you know are the
two important objects of human attention : You
fhall firft fee their ftate and fituation in London.

Inv. You mean the practice of phyfick and law?

Devil. I do. And as to the firft, you will find
it, in fome of the profeffors, a fcience, noble, falutary and liberal ; in others, a trade, as mean as
it is mercenary ; a contemptible combination of
dunces, nurfes, and apothecaries : But you have
now a lucky opportunity of knowing more in an
hour of the great improvements in this branch of
civil fociety, than, by any other means, feven years
could have taught you.

Inv. Explain, if you pleafe.

Devil. The fpirit of Difcord prevails : The
republic of tied periwigs, like the Romans of
old, have turned their arms from the reft of man-
kind, to draw their fhort fwords on themfelves.

Inv. But how came this about?·

Devil. To carry on the metaphor, you muft
know, in this great town, there are two corps of
thefe troops, equally numerous, and equally for-
midable : The firft, it is true, are difciplined, and
fight under a general, whom they chriften a Prefident: The fecond contains the huffars, and pan-
dours of phyfick ; they rarely attacks a patient together;

gether: not but the latter fingle-handed can do good execution.

Inv. But their caufe of contention?

Devil. Pride. The light troops are jealous of fome honours the others poffefs by prefcription, and, though, but a militia, think they have right to an equal rank with the regulars.

Inv. Why, this in time may ruin their ftate.

Devil. True; but that we muft prevent; it is our intereft to make up this breach: Already we feel the fatal effects of their feuds: By neglecting their patients, the weekly bills daily decline, and new fubjects begin to grow fcarce in our realms.

Inv. This does, indeed, claim your attention.

Devil. We purpofe to call in the aid of the law; bleeding the purfe is as effectual for damping the fpirit, as opening a vein for lowering the pulfe: The Dæmon of Litigation has already poffeffed the Licentiates; I muft infufe the fame paffion into the Prefident; and I warrant you, in two or three terms, with two or three trials, all fides will be heartily tired. But, a-propos! I fee a brace of apothecaries coming this way; they feem deep in debate: Let us liften; we fhall beft learn from them the prefent pofture of—Hufh, hide!—You fhall here too have a proof what a Proteus I am.   [*They retire.*

Enter Julep and Apozem, with a letter.

Julep. I tell you, Apozem, you are but young in the bufinefs, and don't forefee how much we fhall be all hurt in the end.

Apozem. Well, but what can be done, Mr. Julep? Here Dr. Hellebore writes me word, that they threaten a fiege, and are provided with

fire-

fire-arms: Would you have them furrender the College at once?

Julep. Fire-arms? If they are mad enough not to know that the pen is the doctor's beft piftol, why, let them proceed!

Apozem. But are we to ftand quietly by, and fee the very feat of the fcience demolifhed and torn?

Julep. And with what arms are we to defend it? where are our cannon? We have mortars indeed, but then they are fit to hold nothing but peftles; and, as to our fmall arms, of what ufe can they be in a fiege? they are made, you know, to attack only the rear.

Apozem. Come, come, Mr. Julep, you make too light of thefe matters: To have the lawful defcendants from Galen, the throne of Efculapius, overturned by a parcel of Goths!

Julep. Peace, Apozem, or treat your betters with proper refpect! What, numfkull, do you think all phyficians are blockheads, who have not wafhed their hands in the Cam or the Ifis?

Apozem. Well, but I hope you will allow that a univerfity-doctor——

Julep. May, for aught you know, be a dunce. Befides, fool, what have we to do with degrees? The doctor that dofes beft is the beft doctor for us. You talk of the College; there are fome of their names, I am fure, that I never defire to fee on my file.

Apozem. Indeed!

Julep. Indeed? no, indeed. Why, there's Dr. Diet, that makes fuch a duft: He had a perfon of fafhion, a patient of mine, under his care t'other day; as fine a flow fever! I was in hopes of half making my fortune——

Apozem.

Apozem. Yes, I love a flow fever. Was it nervous?

Julep. Ay; with a lovely dejection of fpirits.

Apozem. That was delightful, indeed! I look upon the nerves and the bile to be the two beft friends we have to our back.—Well, pray, and how did it anfwer?

Julep. Not at all; the fcoundrel let him flip through my hands for a fong; only a paltry fix pounds and a crown.

Apozem. Shameful!

Julep. Infamous! and yet, forfooth, he was one of your College. Well, now to fhew you the difference in men; but the very week after, Dr. Linctus, from Leyden, run me up a bill of thirty odd pounds, for only attending Alderman Soakpot fix days in a furfeit.

Apozem. Ay, that was doing of bufinefs.

Julep. Ah! that's a fweet pretty practitioner, Apozem: We muft all do our utmoft to pufh him.

Apozem. Without doubt. But, notwithftanding all that you fay, Mr. Julep, there are fome of the gentlemen of the College, that I know——

Julep. Ah! as fine fellows as ever fingered a pulfe; not one of the trade will deny it.

Apozem. But, amongft all now, old Nat Nightfhade is the man for my money.

Julep. Yes; Nat, Nat has merit, I own; but, pox take him! he is fo devilifh quick: To be fure, he has a very pretty fluent pen whilft it lafts; but then he makes fuch difpatch, that one has hardly time to fend in two dozen of draughts.

Apozem. Yes; the doctor drives on, to be fure.

Julep. Drives on! If I am at all free in the houfe when old Nightfhade is fent for, as a preparatory dofe I always recommend an attorney.

Apozem.

Apozem. An attorney? for what?

Julep. To make the patient's will, before he fwallows the doctor's prefcription.

Apozem. That is prudent.

Julep. Yes; I generally afterwards get the thanks of the family.

Apozem. What, Mr. Julep, for the attorney, or the phyfician? ha, ha!

Julep. Ha, ha! you are arch, little Apozem; quite a wag, I profefs.

Apozem. Why, you know, brother Julep, thefe are fubjects upon which one can hardly be ferious.

Julep. True, true; but then you fhould never laugh loud in the ftreet: We may indulge, indeed, a kind of fimpering fmile to our patients, as we drive by in our chariots; but then there is a decency, not to fay dignity, that becomes the publick demeanour of us, who belong to the faculty.

Apozem. True. And yet there are times when one can hardly forbear: Why, t'other day now I had like to have burft: I was following a funeral into St. George's—a fweet pretty burying; velvet pall, hatband and gloves; and, indeed, the widow was quite handfome in all things; paid my bill the next week, without fconcing off fixpence, though they were thought to have lived happily together—but, as I was faying, as we were entering the church, who fhould ftand in the porch but Kit Cabbage the taylor, with a new pair of breeches under his arm: The fly rogue made me a bow, " Servant, mafter Apozem!" fays he; " what you are carrying home your " work too, I fee." Did your ever hear fuch a dog?

Julep.

Julep. Ay, ay; let them, let them—But, is not that Dr. Squib that is croffing the way?

Apozem. Yes; you may fee it is Squib, by his fhuffle. What, I fuppofe now he is fcouring away for the College.

Julep. Who? Squib? how little you know of him! he did not care if all our tribe was tipped into the Thames.

Apozem. No!

Julep. No. Lord help you! he is too much taken up with the national illnefs, to attend to particular ails: Why, he would quit the beft patient in town, to hunt after a political fecret; and would rather have a whifper from a great man in the Court of Requefts, than five hundred pounds for attending him in a chronical cafe.

Apozem. Wonderful!—Who can that dirty boy be that he has in his hand?

Julep. One of his fcouts, I fuppofe.—We fhall fee.

Re-enter Devil, as Dr. Squib, and Printer's Devil.

Squib. And you are fure this was worked off one of the firft?

Boy. Not a fingle one, Sir, has been fent out as yet.

Squib. That is daintily done, my dear devil! Here, child, here's fixpence. When your mafter gives you the reft, you need not be in hafte to deliver them, but ftep into the firft publick-houfe to refrefh you.

Boy. I fhall, Sir.

Squib. By that means, I fhall be earlieft to treat two or three great men that I know with the fight.

Boy. No further commands, Sir?

Squib.

Squib. None, child.—But, d'ye hear? if you can at any time get me the rough reading of any tart political manuſcript, before it goes to the preſs, you ſha'n't be a loſer.

Boy. I ſhall try, Sir.

Squib. That's well! Mind your buſineſs, and go on but as you begin, and I foreſee your fortune is made: Come, who knows but in a little time, if you are a good bóy, you may get yourſelf committed to Newgate.

Boy. Ah, Sir, I am afraid I am too young.

Squib. Not at all: I have ſeen lads in limbo much younger than you. Come, don't be faint-hearted; there has many a printer been raiſed to the pillory from as ſlender beginnings.

Boy. That's great comfort however. Well, Sir, I'll do my endeavour. [*Exit.*

Squib. Do, do!—What, Apozem! Julep! well encountered, my lads! You are a couple of lucky rogues! Here, here's a treat for a prince; ſuch a print, boys! juſt freſh from the plate: Feel it; ſo wet you may ring it.

Julep. And pray, good doctor, what is the ſubject?

Squib. Subject? Gad take me, a trimmer! this will make ſome folks that we know look about them: Hey, Julep, don't you think this will ſting?

Julep. I profeſs I don't underſtand it.

Squib. No? Why, zounds, it is as plain as a pikeſtaff; in your own way too, you blockhead! Can't you ſee? Read, read the title, you rogue! But, perhaps you can't without ſpectacles. Let me ſee; ay, ." The State-Quacks; or, Britannia " Dying:" You take it?

Julep. Very well.

Squib.

Squib. There you fee her ftretched along on a pallet; you may know fhe is Britannia, by the fhield and fpear at the head of her bed.

Apozem. Very plain; for all the world like the wrong fide of a halfpenny!

Squib. Well faid, little Apozem! you have difcernment, I fee. Her difeafe is a lethargy; you fee how fick fhe is, by holding her hand to her head; don't you fee that?

Julep. I do, I do.

Squib. Well then, look at that figure there upon her left-hand.

Julep. Which?

Squib. Why, he that holds a draught to her mouth.

Julep. What, the man with the phial?

Squib. Ay, he! he with the phial: That is fuppofed to be—[*whifpers*.] offering her laudanum, to lull her fafter afleep.

Julep. Laudanum! a noble medicine when adminiftered properly: I remember once, in a locked jaw——

Squib. Damn your lock'd jaw! hold your prating, you puppy! I wifh your jaws were lock'd! Pox take him, I have forgot what I was going to —Apozem, where did I leave off?

Apozem. You left off at fafter afleep.

Squib. True; I was at fafter afleep. Well then; you fee that thin figure there, with the meagre chaps; he with the ftraw in his hand.

Apozem. Very plain.

Squib. He is fuppofed to be——[*whifpers*] You take me?

Julep. Ay, ay.

Squib. Who rouzes Britannia, by tickling her nofe with that ftraw; fhe ftarts, and with a jerk—

[ftarting,

[*ftarting, ftrikes Julep.*] I beg pardon!—and with a jerk knocks the bottle of laudanum out of his hand; and fo, by that there means, you fee, Britannia is delivered from death.

Julep. Ay, ay.

Squib. Hey! you fwallow the fatire; Pretty bitter, I think?

Julep. I can't fay that I quite underftand—that is—a—a—

Squib. Not underftand? then what a fool am I to throw away my time on a dunce! I fhall mifs too the reading a new pamphlet in Red-Lyon-Square; and at fix I muft be at Serjeant's-Inn, to juftify bail for a couple of journeymen printers.

Apozem. But, Dr. Squib, you feem to have forgot the cafe of the College, your brethren.

Squib. I have no time to attend their trifling fquabbles: The nation, the nation, Mr. Apozem, engroffes my care. The College! could they but get me a ftiptic to ftop the bleeding wounds of my—it is there, there, that I feel! Oh, Julep, Apozem,

> Could they but caft the water of this land,
> Purge her grofs humours, purify her blood,
> And give her back her priftine health again,
> I would applaud them to the very echo
> That fhould appland again!

Julep. Indeed, Dr. Squib, that I believe is out of the way of the College.

> *Squib.* Throw phyfic to the dogs then! I'll have none of't.
> But tell me, Apozem, inform me, Julep,
> What fenna, rhubarb, or what purgative drug,
> Can fcour thefe——hence?

You underftand me, lads!

Julep. In good truth, not I, Sir.

Squib.

Squib. No! then fo˙ much the better! I warrant little Pozy does.—Well, adieu, my brave boys! for I have not an inftant to lofe. Not underftand me, hey? Apozem, you do, you rogue?—

What fenna, rhubarb, or—hey—can fcour thefe Se—

Egad, I had like to have gone too far!—Well, bye, bye!   [*Exit Squib.*

Julep. Why, the poor man feems out of his fenfes.

Apozem. When he talked of throwing phyfic to the dogs, I confefs I began to fufpect him. But we fhall be late; we muft attend our fummons, you know.

Julep. Throw phyfic to the dogs! I can tell thee, Apozem, if he does not get cured of thefe fancies and freaks, he is more likely to go to the kennel by half. Throw phyfic to the dogs! an impertinent ignorant puppy!   [*Exeunt.*

    Re enter Devil, Invoice, and Harriet.

Devil. Well, I think chance has thrown a pretty good fample into your way. Now, if I could but get one to conduct you—But ftay! who have we here?

    Enter Laft, with a pair of fhoes.

Laft. Pray, good gentleman, can you tell a body which is the ready road to find Warwick-lane?

Devil. Warwick-lane, friend? and prithee what can thy errand be there?

Laft. I am going there to take out a licence to make me a doctor, an like your worfhip.

Devil. Where do you live?

Laft. A little way off, in the country.

C

Devil.

Devil. Your name, honeſt friend, and your
buſineſs?

Laſt. My name, maſter, is Laſt; by trade I
am a doctor, and by profeſſion a maker of ſhoes :
I was born to the one, and bred up to the other.

Devil. Born? I don't underſtand you.

Laſt. Why, I am a ſeventh ſon, and ſo were
my father.

Devil. Oh! a very clear title. And pray, now,
in what branch does your ſkill chiefly lie ?

Laſt. By caſting a water, I cures the jaundarſe ;
I taps folks for a tenpenny; and have a choice
charm for the agar ; and, over and above that,
maſter, I bleeds.

Devil. Bleeds? and are your neighbours ſo bold
as to truſt you ?

Laſt. Truſt me? ay, maſter, that they will,
ſooner than narra a man in the country. May-
hap you may know Dr. Tyth'em, our rector at
home.

Devil. I can't ſay that I do.

Laſt. He's the flower of a man in the pulpit.
Why, t'other day, you muſt know, taking a turn
in his garden, and thinking of nothing at all,
down falls the doctor flat in a fit of perplexity ;
Madam Tyth'em, believing her huſband was
dead, directly ſent the ſexton for I.

Devil. An affectionate wife !

Laſt. Yes; they are a main happy couple.
Sure as a gun, maſter, when I comed, his face
was as black as his caſſock : But, howſomdever,
I took out my launcelot, and forthwith opened a
large artifice here in one of the juglers : The
doctor bled like a pig.

Devil. I dare ſay.

Laſt.

Laſt. But it did the buſineſs, howſomdever; I compaſſed the job.

Devil. What, he recovered?

Laſt. Recovered? Lord help you! why, but laſt Sunday was ſe'nnight—to be ſure, the doctor is given to weeze a little—becauſe why, he is main opulent, and apt to be tiſicky—but he compoſed as ſweet a diſcourſe—I ſlept from beginning to end.

Devil. That was compoſing, indeed.

Laſt. Ay, warn't it, maſter, for a man that is ſtrucken in years?

Devil. Oh, a wonderful effort!

Laſt. Well, like your worſhip, and, beſides all this I have been telling you, I have a pretty tight hand at a tooth.

Devil. Indeed!

Laſt. Ay, and I'll ſay a bold word, that, in drawing a thouſand, I. never ſtumpt a man in my life: Now, let your Raſperini's, and all your foreign mounſeers, with their fine dainty freeches, ſay the like if they can.

Devil. I defy them.

Laſt. So you may. Then, about a dozen years ago, before theſe here Suttons made ſuch a noiſe, I had ſome thoughts of occupying for the ſmall-pox.

Devil. Ay; that would have wound up your bottom at once. And, why did not you?

Laſt. Why, I don't know, maſter; the neighbours were frightful, and would not conſent; otherwiſe, by this time, 'tis my belief, men, women, and children, I might have occupied twenty thouſand at leaſt.

Devil. Upon my word!—But, you ſay a dozen years, maſter Laſt: As you have practiſed phyſic

C 2 ·   without

without permiſſion ſo long, what makes you now think of getting a licence?

Laſt. Why, it is all along with one Lotion, a pottercarrier, that lives in a little town hard by we; he is grown old and laſcivious, I think, and threatens to preſent me at ſize, if ſo be I practize any longer.

Devil. What, I ſuppoſe you run away with the buſineſs?

Laſt. Right, maſter, you have gueſſed the matter at once. So I was telling my tale to Sawney M'Gregor, who comes now and then to our town with his pack; God, he adviſed me to get made a doctor at once, and ſend for a diplummy from Scotland.

Devil. Why, that was the right road, maſter Laſt.

Laſt. True. But my maſter Tyth'em tells me, that I can get it done for pretty near the ſame price here in London: ſo, I had rather, d'ye ſee, lay out my money at home, than tranſport it to foreign parts, as we ſay; becauſe why, maſter, I thinks there has too much already gone that road.

Devil. Spoke like an Engliſhman!

Laſt. I have a pair of ſhoes here, to carry home to farmer Fallow's ſon, that lives with maſter Grogram the mercer, hard by here in Cheapſide; ſo I thought I might as well do both buſineſſes under one.

Devil. True. Your way, maſter Laſt, lies before you; the ſecond ſtreet, you muſt turn to the left; then enter the firſt great gates that you ſee.

Laſt. And who muſt I aks for?

Devil. Oh, pull out your purſe; you will find that hint ſufficient: It is a part of the world where a fee is never refuſed.

Laſt.

Laſt. Thank you, maſter! You are main kind; very civil indeed! [*Going, returns.*] I wiſh, maſter, you had now either the agar or jaundarſe; I would ſet you right in a trice.

Devil. Thank you, maſter Laſt; but I am as well as I am.

Laſt. Or, if ſo be you likes to open a vein, or would have a tooth or two knocked out of your head, I'll do it for nothing.

Devil. Not at preſent, I thank you! when I want, I'll call at your houſe in the country.

[*Exit Laſt.*

Well, my young couple, and what ſay you now?

Inv. Say, Sir? that I am more afraid of being ſick than ever I was in my life.

Devil. Pho! you know nothing as yet. But, my time draws nigh for poſſeſſing the Preſident: If I could but get but ſome intelligent perſon, to conduct you to the place where the Licentiates aſſemble—There ſeems a ſober, ſedate-looking lad; perhaps he may anſwer our purpoſe. Hark'e, young man!

Enter Johnny Macpherſon.

Macp. What's your wul, Sir? would you ſpear aught wi me?

Devil. Though I think I can give a good gueſs, pray from what part of the world may you come?

Macp. My name is Johnny Macpherſon, and I came out of the North.

Devil. Are you in buſineſs at preſent?

Macp. I conna ſay that, Sir, nor that I am inteerely daſtitute neither; but I ſal be unco glad to get a mair ſolid eſtaabliſhment.

Devil. Have you been long in this town?

C 3

Macp.

Macp. Aboot a month awa, Sir: I launded fra Leith, in the gude ship the Traquair, Davy Donaldson maifter, and am lodged wi Sawney Sinclair, at the fign o' the Ceety of Glafcow, not far fra the Monument.

Devil. But you are in employment?

Macp. Ay, for fome paart of the day.

Devil. And to what may your profits amount?

Macp. Ah! for the mater of that, it is a praty fmart little income.

Devil. Is it a fecret how much?

Macp. Not at aw : I get three-pence an hour for larning Latin to a phyfician in the ceety.

Devil. The very man that we want.—Latin! and, what, are you capable?

Macp. Cappable! Hut awa, mon! Ken ye, that I was heed of the humanity-clafs for mair than a twalvemonth? and was offered the chair of the gramatical profefforfhip in the College, which amunts to a mater of fux pounds Britifh a-year.

Devil. That's more than I knew. Can you guefs, Sir, where your fcholar is now?

Macp. It is na long, Sir, that I laft him conning his *As in præfenti*; after which, he talked of ganging to meet fome freends o' the faculty, aboot a fort of a fquabble, that he fays is fprang up among them; he wanted me to gang along wi him; as I had gi'n myfel to ftudy madicine a little, before I quitted the North.

Devil. Do you know the publick-houfe where they meet?

Macp. Yes, yes, unco weel, Sir; it is at the tavern the South fide of Paul's Kirk.

Devil. Will you take the trouble to conduct this young couple thither? they will amply reward you.

you.—You and your partner will follow this lad. Fear nothing! by my art, you are invisible to all but those that you desire should see you. At the College we shall rejoin one another; for thither the Licentiates will lead you.

Inv. But how shall we be able to distinguish you from the rest of the Fellows?

Devil. By my large wig, and superior importance; in a word, you must look for me in the PRESIDENT.

Inv. Adieu.   [*Exeunt.*

ACT III.

SCENE A STREET.

Fingerfee, Sligo, Osasafras, Broadbrim, other Doctors, and Macpherson, discovered.

Fingerfee.

NO; I can't help thinking this was by much the best method. If, indeed, they refuse us an amicable entrance, we are then justified in the use of corrosives.

Sligo. I tell you, Dr. Fingerfee—I am sorry, d'ye see, to differ from so old a practitioner; but I don't like your prescription at all, at all: For what signifies a palliative regiment, with such a rotten constitution? May I never finger a pulse as long as I live, if you get their voluntary consent to go in, unless indeed it be by compulsion.

Osaf. I entirely coincide with my very capable countryman, Dr. Sligo, d'ye see; and do give my advice, in this consultation, for putting the whole College under a course of steel, without further delay.

Sligo. I am much obligated to you for your kind compliment, doctor. But, pray, what may your name be?

Ofaf. Dr. Ofafafras, at your humble fervice.

Sligo. I am your very obadient alfho! I have hard tell of your name. But what did you mane by my countryman? Pray, doctor, of what nation are you?

Ofaf. Sir, I have the honour to be a native of Ireland.

Sligo. Ofafafras? that's a name of no note; he is not a Milefian, I am fure. The family, I fuppofe, came over t'other day with Strongbow, not above feven or eight hundred years ago; or perhaps a defcendant from one of Oliver's drummers.—'Pon my confcience, doctor, I fhould hardly belave you were Irifh.

Ofaf. What, Sir, d'ye doubt my veracity?

Sligo. Not at all, my dear doctor; it is not for that: But, between me and yourfelf, you have lived a long time in this town.

Ofaf. Like enough.

Sligo. Ay; and was here a great while before ever I faw it.

Ofaf. What of that?

Sligo. Very well, my dear doctor: Then, putting that and t'other together, my notion of the upfhot is, that if fo be you are a native of Ireland, upon my confcience, you muft have been born there very young.

Ofaf. Young? ay, to be fure: Why, my foul, I was chriftened there.

Sligo. Ay!

Ofaf. Ay, was I, in the county of Meath.

Sligo. Oh, that alters the property; that makes it as clear as Fleet-Ditch. I fhould be glad,

countryman,

countryman, of your nearer acquaintance.—
But what little flim doctor is that, in his own
head of hair? I don't recollect to have feen his
features before.

Ofaf. Nor I, to my knowledge.

Sligo Perhaps he may be able to tell me, if I
aks him himfelf.—I am proud to fee you, doctor,
on this occoafion; becaafe why, it becomes every
jontleman that is of the faculty—that is, that
is not of their faculty; you underftand me—to
look about him and ftir.

Macp. Oh, by my troth, you are right, Sir;
The leemiting of phyfic aw to ain hoofe, caw it
a College, or by what denomination you wul, it
is at beft but eftaablifhing a fort of monopoly.

Sligo. 'Pon my confcience, that is a fine obfer-
vation. By the twift of your tongue, doctor,
(no offence) I fhould be apt to guefs that you
might be a foreigner born?

Macp. Sir!

Sligo. From Ruffia, perhaps, or Mufcovy?

Macp. Hut awa, mon! not at aw: Zounds, I
am a Breeton.

Sligo. Then, I fhould fuppofe, doctor, pretty
far to the northward.

Macp. Ay; your are right, Sir.

Sligo. And pray, doctor, what particular
branch of our bufinefs may have taken up the
moft of your time?

Macp. Botany.

Sligo. Botany! in what college?

Macp. The univerfity of St, Andrews.

Ofaf. Pray, doctor, is not botany a very dry
fort of a ftudy?

Sligo. Moft damnably fo in thofe parts, my
dear doctor; for all the knowledge they have
they

they muſt get from dried herbs, becaaſe the devil of any green that will grow there.

Macp. Sir, your information is wrong.

Sligo. Come, my dear doctor, · hold your palaver, and don't be after puffing on us, becaaſe why, you know in your conſcience that in your part of the world you get no cabbage but thiſtles ; and thoſe you are obliged to raiſe upon hot-beds.

Macp. Thiſtles! zounds, Sir, d'ye mean to affront me?

Sligo. That, doctor, is as you plaaſes to taake it.

Macp. God's life, Sir, I would ha' you to ken, that there is narra a mon wi his heed upon his ſhoulders that dare——

Fing. Peace, peace, gentlemen! let us have no civil diſcord. Doctor Sligo is a lover of pleaſantry; but, I am ſure, had no deſign to affront you: A joke, nothing elſe.

Macp. A joke! ah; I like a joke weel enough; but I did na underſtond the doctor's gibing and geering: Perhaps my wut may not be aw together as ſharp as the doctor's, but I have a ſword, Sir——

Sligo. A ſword, Sir!

Fing. A ſword! ay, ay; there is no doubt but you have both very good ones ; but reſerve them for—Oh! here comes our ambaſſador.

Enter .Diachylon.

Well, Dr. Diachylon, what news from the College? will they allow us free ingreſs and egreſs?

Diac. I could not get them to ſwallow a ſingle demand.

All. No?

Sligo.

Sligo. Then let us drive there, and drench them.

Diac. I was heard with difdain, and refufed with an air of defiance.

Sligo. There, gentlemen! I foretold you what would happen at firft.

All. He did, he did.

Sligo. Then we have nothing for it, but to force our paffage at once.

All. By all means; let us march!

Broad. Friend Fingerfee, would our brethren but incline their ears to me for a minute—

Fing. Gentlemen, Dr. Broadbrim defires to be heard.

All. Hear him, hear him!

Sligo. Paw, honey, what fignifies hearing? I long to be doing, my jewel!

Fing. But hear Dr. Melchifedech Broadbrim, however.

All. Ay, ay; hear Dr. Broadbrim!

Broad. Fellow-labourers in the fame vineyard! ye know well how much I ftand inclined to our caufe; forafmuch as not one of my brethren can be more zealous than I——

All. True, true.

Broad. But ye wot alfo, that I hold it not meet or wholfome to ufe a carnal weapon, even for the defence of myfelf; much more unfeemly then muft I deem it to draw the fword for the offending of others.

Sligo. Paw! brother doctors, don't let him bother us, with his *yea* and *nay* nonfenfe!

Broad. Friend Sligo, do not be cholerick; and know, that I am as free to draw my purfe in this caufe, as thou art thy fword: And thou wilt

wilt find, at the length, notwithftanding thy
fwaggering, that the firft will do us beft fervice.

Sligo. Well, but—

All. Hear him, hear him!

Broad. It is my notion, then, brethren, that
we do forthwith fend for a finful man in the
flefh, called an attorney.

Sligo. An attorney!

Broad. Ay, an attorney; and that we do direct
him to take out a parchment inftrument, with a
feal fixed thereto.

Sligo. Paw, pox! what good can that do?

Broad. Don't be too hafty, friend Sligo.—
And therewith, I fay, let him poffefs the out-
ward tabernacle of the vain man, · who de-
lighteth to call himfelf Prefident, and carry him
before the men cloathed in lambfkin, who at
Weftminfter are now fitting in judgment.

Sligo. Paw! a law-fuit! that won't end with
our lives.—Let us march!

All. Ay, ay.

Sligo. Come, Dr. Habakkuk, will you march
in the front or the rear?

Hab. Pardon me, doctor! I cannot attend
you.

Sligo. What, d'ye draw back, when it comes
to the pufh?

Hab. Not at all; I would gladly join in
putting thefe Philiftines to flight! for I abhor
them worfe than hogs' puddings, in which the
unclean beaft and the blood are all jumbled
together.

Sligo. Pretty food, for all that.

Hab. But this is Saturday; and I dare not
draw my fword on the Sabbath.

Sligo.

Sligo. Then ſtay with your brother Melchi-
ſedech; for, though of different religions, you are
both of a kidney. Come, doctors; out with
your ſwords! Huzza! and now for the Lane!
Huzza!   [*Exeunt.*

Manent Broadbrim and Habakkuk.

Broad. Friend Habakkuk, thou ſeeſt how
headſtrong and wilful theſe men are: but let
us uſe diſcretion, however. Wilt thou ſtep to
the Inn that taketh its name from the city of
Lincoln? enquire there for a man, with a red
rag at his back, a ſmall black cap on his pate,
and a buſhel of hair on his breaſt? I think they
call him a ſerjeant.

Hab. They do.

Broad. Then, without let or delay, bring him
hither, I pray thee.

Hab. I will about it this inſtant.

Broad. His admonition, perhaps, may prevail. Uſe diſpatch, I beſeech thee, friend Habakkuk.

Hab. As much as if I was poſting to the Trea-
ſury, to obtain a large ſubſcription in a new
loan, or a lottery.

Broad. Nay, then, friend, I have no reaſon to
fear thee.   [*Exeunt*

THE COLLEGE.

*Devil (as Hellebore, the Preſident) Camphire, Calomel
Secretary, and Pupils, diſcovered.*

Sec. The Licentiates, Sir, will ſoon be at hand.

Hel. Let them!

Cal. We will do our duty, however; and,
like the patricians of old, receive with ſilence
theſe Viſigoths in the ſenate.

Hel.

Hel. I am not, Dr. Calomel, of so pacific a turn: Let us keep the evil out of doors, if we can; if not, *vim vi*, repel force by force.—Barricado the gates!

Sec. It is done.

Hel. Are the buckets and fire-engine fetched from St. Dunstan's?

Sec. They have been here, Sir, this half-hour.

Hel. Let twelve apothecaries be placed at the pump, and their apprentices supply 'em with water!

Sec. Yes, Sir.

Hel. But let the engine be play'd by old Jollup, from James-street! Not one of the trade has a better hand at directing a pipe.

Sec. Mighty well, Sir.

Hel. In the time of siege, every citizen ought in duty to serve.—Having thus, brothers, provided a proper defence, let us coolly proceed to our business. Is there any body here, to demand a licence to-day?

Sec. A practitioner, Mr. President, out of the country.

Hel. Are the customary fees all discharged?

Sec. All, Sir.

Hel. Then let our censors, Dr. Christopher Camphire, and Dr. Cornelius Calomel, introduce the petitioner for examination.

　　　　　　[*Exeunt Camphire and Calomel.*
After this duty is dispatch'd, we will then read the College and Students a lecture.

　　　Enter Camphire and Calomel, with Last.

Last. First, let me lay down my shoes.
　　　[*They advance, with three bows, to the table.*
　　　　　　　　　　　　　　　　Hel.

Hel. Let the candidate be placed on a ftool.
What's the doctor's name?

Sec. Emanuel Laft, Mr. Prefident.

Hel. Dr. Laft, you have petitioned the College, to obtain a licence for the practice of
phyfic; and though we have no doubt of your
great fkill and abilities, yet our duty compels us
previoufly to afk a few queftions: What academy had the honour to form you?

Laft. Anan!

Hel. We want to know the name of the place,
where you have ftudied the fcience of phyfic.

Laft. Dunftable.

Hel. That's fome German univerfity; fo he
can never belong to the College.

All. Never; oh, no

Hel. Now, Sir, with regard to your phyfiological knowledge. By what means, Dr. Laft,
do you difcover that a man is not well?

Laft. By his complaint that he is ill.

Hel. Well replied! no furer prognoftic.

All. None furer.

Hel. Then, as to recovering a fubject that is
ill—Can you venture to undertake the cure of
an ague?

Laft. With arra a man in the country.

Hel. By what means?

Laft. By a charm.

Hel. And pray of what materials may that
charm be compofed?

Laft. I won't tell; 'tis a fecret.

Hel. Well replied! the College has no right
to pry into fecrets.

All. Oh, no; by no means.

Hel. But now, Dr. Laft, to proceed in due
form; are you qualified to adminifter remedies
to fuch difeafes as belong to the head?

Laft.

Laſt. I believe I may.

Hel. Name ſome to the College.

Laſt. The tooth-ache.

Hel. What do you hold the beſt method to treat it?

Laſt. I pulls 'em up by the ròots.

Hel. Well replied, brothers! that, without doubt, is a radical cure.

All. Without doubt.

Hel. Thus far as to the head: Proceed we next to the middle! When, Dr. Laſt, you are called in to a patient with a pain in his bowels, what then is your method of practice?

Laſt. I claps a trencher hot to the part.

Hel. Embrocation; very well! But if this application ſhould fail, what is the next ſtep that you take? /

Laſt. I gi's a vomit and a purge.

Hel. Well replied! for it is plain there is a diſagreeable gueſt in the houſe; he has opened both doors; if he will go out at neither, it is none of his fault.

All. Oh, no; by no means.

Hel. We have now diſpatched the middle and head: Come we finally to the other extremity, the feet! Are you equally ſkilful in the diſorders incidental to them?

Laſt. I believe I may.

Hel. Name ſome.

Laſt. I have a great vogue all our way for curing of corns.

Hel. What are the means that you uſe?

Laſt. I cuts them out.

Hel. Well replied! extirpation: No better method of curing can be. Well, brethren, I think we may now, after this ſtrict and impar-

tial

tial enquiry, fafely certify, that Dr. Laft, from
top to toe, is an able phyfician.

All. Very able, very able, indeed.

Hel. And every way qualified to proceed, in
his practice.

All. Every way qualified.

Hel. You may defcend, Dr. Laft. [*Laft takes
his feat among them.*] Secretary, firft read, and
then give the doctor his licence.

Sec. [*Reads.*] " To all whom thefe prefents
may come greeting. Know, ye, that, after a
moft ftrict and fevere inquifition, not only into
the great fkill and erudition, but the morals of
Dr. Emanual Laft, We are authorized to grant
unto the faid doctor full power, permiffion, and
licence, to pill, bolus, lotion, potion, draught,
dofe, drench, purge, bleed, blifter, clifter, cup,
fcarify, fyringe, falivate, couch, flux, fweat,
diet, dilute, tap, plaifter, and poultice, all perfons, in all difeafes, of all ages, conditions, and
fexes. And we do ftrictly command and enjoin
all furgeons, apothecaries, with their apprentices, all midwives, male, female, and nurfes,
at all times, to be aiding and affifting to the faid
Dr. Emanuel Laft. And we do further charge
all mayors, juftices, aldermen, fheriffs, bailiffs,
headboroughs, conftables, and coroners, not to
moleft or intermeddle with the faid doctor, if any
party whom he fhall fo pill, bolus, lotion, potion, draught, dofe, drench, purge, bleed, blifter,
clifter, cup, fcarify, fyringe, falivate, couch,
flux, fweat, diet, dilute, tap, plaifter, and poultice, fhould happen to die, but to deem that the
faid party died a natural death, any thing ap-
pearing to the contrary notwithftanding. Given

D   under

under our hands, &c. Hercules Hellebore,
Cornelius Calomel, Chriſtopher Camphire.

Laſt. Then, if a patient die, they muſt not
ſay that I kill'd him?

Hel. They ſay! Why, how ſhould they know,
when it is not one time in twenty that we know
it ourſelves?—Proceed we now to the lecture!
[*They all riſe and come forward to the table.*] Brethren, and ſtudents, I am going to open to you
ſome notable diſcoveries that I have made, re-
ſpecting the ſource, or primary cauſe, of all diſ-
tempers incidental to the human machine: And
theſe, brethren, I attribute to certain animalculæ,
or piſcatory entities, that inſinuate themſelves
thro' the pores into the blood, and in that fluid
ſport, toſs, and tumble about, like mackrel or
cod-fiſh in the great deep: And to convince you
that this is not a mere *gratis dictum*, an hypo-
theſis only, I will give you demonſtrative proof.
Bring hither the microſcope!

Enter a Servant with a microſcope.

Doctor Laſt, regard this receiver. Take a peep.

Laſt. Where?

Hel. There. Thoſe two yellow drops there
were drawn from a ſubject afflicted with the
jaundice.—Well, what d'ye ſee?

Laſt. Some little creatures like yellow flies,
that are hopping and ſkipping about.

Hel. Right. Thoſe yellow flies give the tinge
to the ſkin, and undoubtedly cauſe the diſeaſe:
And, now, for the cure! I adminiſter to every
patient the two-and-fiftieth part of a ſcruple of
the ovaria or eggs of the ſpider; theſe are thrown
by the digeſtive powers into the ſecretory, there
ſeparated

feparated from the alimentóry, and then preci-
pitated into the circulatory; where finding a proper nidus, or neft, they quit their torpid ftate,
and vivify, and, upon vivification, difcerning
the flies, their natural food, they immediately
fall foul of them, extirpate the race out of
the blood, and reftore the patient to health.

Laft. And what becomes of the fpiders?

Hel. Oh, they die, you know, for want of
nutrition. Then I fend the patient down to
Brighthelmftone; and a couple of dips in the
falt-water wafhes the cobwebs entirely out of
the blood. Now, gentlemen, with refpect to
the——

Enter Servant.

Serv. Sir, Mr. Forceps, from the Hofpital.

Hel. The Hofpital! is this a time to——

Enter Forceps.

Well, Forceps, what's your will?

For. To know, Sir, what you would have done
with the Hofpital patients to-day?

Hel. To-day! why, what was done yefterday?

For. Sir, we bled the Weft ward, and jalloped
the North.

Hel. Did ye? why then, bleed the North ward,
and jallop the Weft to-day. [*Exit For.*
Now, I fay, brethren——

Enter Servant.

Serv. The Licentiates are drawn up at the
gate.

Hel. Who leads 'em?

D 2 *Serv.*

Serv. They are led on by Sligo: They demand inftant entrance, and threaten to ftorm.

Hel. Doctors Calomel and Camphire, our two aid-de camps, furvey their prefent pofture, and report it to us.

Without. Huzza!

Hel. Bid old Jollup be ready to unmafk the engine at the word of command.

Enter Camphire.

Hel. Now, Dr. Camphire?

Camp. The fledge-hammers are come, and they prepare to batter in breach.

Hel. Let the engine be play'd off at the very firft blow!   [*Exit Camp.*

Without. Huzza!

Enter Calomel.

Hel. Now, doctor?

Cal. The firft fire has demolifhed Dr. Fingerfee's foretop.

Hel. That's well.   [*Exit Cal.*

Enter Camphire.

Now, doctor?

Camp. The fecond fire has dropped the ftiff buckles of Dr. Ofafafras.

Hel. Better and better!   [*Exit Camp.*

Enter Calomel.

Now, doctor?

Cal. Both the knots of Dr. Anodyne's tye are diffolved.

Hel. Beft of all!   [*Exit Cal.*
Enter

Enter Camphire.

Now, doctor?

Camp. As Dr. Sligo, with open mouth, drove furiously on, he received a full stream in his teeth, and is retired from the field, dropping wet.

Hel. Then the day's our own!   [*Exit Camp.*

Enter Calomel.

Now, doctor?

Cal. All is lost! Dr. Sligo, recruited by a bumper of Drogheda, is returned with fresh vigour.

Hel. Let our force be pointed at him.

[*Exit Cal.*

Enter Camphire.

Now, doctor?

Camp. The siege slackens; Dr. Broadbrim, with serjeant Demur, are arrived in the camp.

[*Exit.*

Hel. What can that mean?

Enter Calomel.

Now, doctor?

Cal. Serjeant Demur has thrown this manifesto over the gate.   [*Exit.*

Hel. [*looking at the parchment.*] Ha! " Middle-" sex to wit. John Doe and Richard Roe." It is a challenge to meet 'em at Westminster-Hall; then we have breathing-time till the term.

Enter Last.

Now, doctor?

D 3

I. 1.

Laſt. I have forgot my ſhoes.

[*Takes them up, and exit.*

Hel. Oh !

Enter Camphire.

Camp. The Licentiates file off towards Fleet Street.

Hel Follow all, and harraſs the rear! leave not a dry thread among them! Huzza! [*Exeunt.*

Re-enter Devil, Invoice, and Harriet.

Devil. Well, my young friends, you will now be naturally led to Weſtm—Oh!

Inv. Bleſs me, Sir, what's the matter? You change colour, and falter.

Devil. The magician at Madrid has diſcovered my flight, and recalls me by an irreſiſtible ſpell: I muſt leave you, my friends!

Inv. Forbid it, Fortune! it is now, Sir, that we moſt want your aid.

Devil. He muſt, he will be obeyed. Hereafter, perhaps, I may rejöin you again.

Inv. But, Sir, what can we do? how live? what plan can we fix on for our future ſupport?

Devil. You are in a country where your talents, with a little application, will procure you a proviſion.

Inv. But which way to direct them?

Devil. There are profitable profeſſions, that require but little ability.

Inv. Name us one.

Devil. What think you of the trade with whoſe badge I am at preſent inveſted?

Inv. Can you ſuppoſe, Sir, after what I have ſeen——

Devil.

Devil. Oh, Sir, I don't defign to engage you in any perfonal fervice; I would only recommend it to you to be the vender of fome of thofe infallible remedies, with which our newfpapers are conftantly crouded?

Inv. You know, Sir, I am poffeffed of no fecret.

Devil. Nor they either: A few fimple waters, dignified with titles that catch, no matter how wild and abfurd, will effectually anfwer your purpofe: As, let me fee now! Tincture of Tinder, Effence of Eggfhell, or Balfam of Broomftick.

Inv. You muft excufe me, Sir; I can never fubmit.

Devil. I think you are rather too fqueamifh. What fay you, then, to a little fpiritual quackery?

Inv. Spiritual?

Devil. Oh, Sir, there are in this town mountebanks for the mind, as well as the body. How fhould you like mounting a cart on a common, and becoming a Methodift Preacher?

Inv. Can that fcheme turn to account?

Devil. Nothing better: Believe me, the abfolute direction of the perfons and purfes of a large congregation, however low their conditions and callings, is by no means a contemptible object. I, for my own part, can fay, what the Conqueror of Perfia faid to the Cynic; "If " I was not Alexander, I would be Diogenes:" So, if I was not the Devil, I would chufe to be a Methodift Preacher.

Inv. But then the reftraint, the forms, I fhall be obliged to obferve.

Devil. None at all: There is, in the whole catalogue, but one fin you need be at all fhy of committing.

Inv.

Inv. What's that?

Devil. Simony.

Inv. Simony! I don't comprehend you.

Devil. Simony, Sir, is a new kind of canon, devifed by thefe upftart fanatics, that makes it finful not to abufe the confidence, and pioufly plunder the little property, of an indigent man, and his family.

Inv. A moft noble piece of cafuiftical cookery, and exceeds even the fons of Ignatius! But this honour I muft beg to decline.

Devil. What think you then of trying the ftage? You are a couple of good theatrical figures; but how are your talents? can you fing?

Inv. I can't boaft of much fkill, Sir; but Mifs Harriet got great reputation in Spain.

Har. Oh, Mr. Invoice! My father, Sir, as we feldom went out, eftablifhed a domeftic kind of drama, and made us perform fome little mufical pieces, that were occafionally fent us from England.

Devil. Come, Sir, will you give us a tafte of your—juft a fhort—*te ti te tor.*

[*Sings a fhort preludio.*

Inv. I muft beg to be excufed, Sir; I have not a mufical note in my voice, that can pleafe you.

Devil. No? Why then, I believe we muft trouble the lady: Come, Mifs, I'll charm a band to accompany you.   [*Waves his ftick.*

[*Harriet fings.*]

Devil. Exceedingly well! You have nothing to do now, but to offer yourfelves to one of the houfes.

Inv.

Inv. And which, Sir, would you recommend ?

Devil. Take you choice ; for I can ferve you in neither.

Inv. No? I thought, Sir, you told me juft now, that the feveral arts of the drama were under your direction.

Devil. So they were formerly; but now they are directed by the Genius of Infipidity: He has entered into partnerfhip with the managers of both houfes, and they have fet up a kind of circulating library, for the vending of dialogue novels. I dare not go near the new houfe, for the Dæmon of Power, who gave me this lame-nefs, has poffeffed the pates, and fown difcord among the mock monarchs there ; and what one receives, the other rejects. And as to the other houfe, the manager has great merit himfelf, with fkill to difcern, and candor to allow it in others ; but I can be of no ufe in making your bargain, for in that he would be too many for the cunningeft Devil amongft us.

Inv. I have heard of a new playhoufe in the Haymarket.

Devil. What, Foote's? Oh, that's an eccentric, narrow eftablifhment; a mere fummer fly ! He ! But, however, it may do for a *coup d'effai,* and prove no bad foundation for a future engage-ment.

Inv. Then we will try him, if you pleafe.

Devil. By all means : And you may do it this inftant; he opens to-night, and will be glad of your affiftance. I'll drop you down at the door ; and muft then take my leave for fome time. *Allons!* but don't tremble; you have nothing to

fear:

fear: The public will treat you with kindnefs;
at leaft, if they fhew but half the indulgence to
you, that they have upon all occafions fhewn to
that Manager.   [*Exeunt omnes.*

F I N I S.